D1272523

# Out and About at the BASEBALL STADIUM

by Bitsy Kemper
illustrated by Zachary Trover

Special thanks to our advisers for their expertise:

Tony Asaro, Senior Director of Community Relations
Sacramento River Cats Baseball Club

Susan Kesselring, M.A., Literacy Educator
Rosemount–Apple Valley–Eagan (Minnesota) School District

**PICTURE WINDOW BOOKS**
Minneapolis, Minnesota

*To my husband, Vince, the coolest stadium fan I know!–BK*

Editor: Nick Healy
Designer: Tracy Kaehler
Page Production: Lori Bye
Creative Director: Keith Griffin
Editorial Director: Carol Jones
The illustrations in this book were created digitally.

Picture Window Books
5115 Excelsior Boulevard
Suite 232
Minneapolis, MN 55416
877-845-8392
www.picturewindowbooks.com

Printed in the United States of America.

**Library of Congress Cataloging-in-Publication Data**
Kemper, Bitsy.
Out and about at the baseball stadium / by Bitsy Kemper ; illustrated by Zachary Trover.
p. cm. — (Field trips)
Includes bibliographical references.
ISBN-13: 978-1-4048-2280-1 (hardcover)
ISBN-10: 1-4048-2280-1 (hardcover)
1. Stadiums—United States—Juvenile literature. 2. Sports facilities—United States—Juvenile
literature. I. Trover, Zachary. II. Title. III. Series: Field trips (Picture Window Books)
GV415.K46 2006
796'.068—dc22                                          2006003526

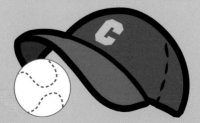

We're going on a field trip to a baseball stadium. We can't wait!

Things to find out:

How many people do stadiums hold?

What is a clubhouse?

What happens in the training room?

Who works in the press box?

Hi, everyone. My name is Pete, and I work in the front office here at Kemper Baseball Stadium. Let's get started on our tour.

A baseball stadium is a huge building. This stadium covers 20 acres (8 hectares). That's about the same area as 18 football fields! There are 40,000 seats in here—enough for a small city.

TICKETS

COMETS

4

With so many people attending games, stadiums need large parking lots. Some parking lots are big enough to fit eight stadiums.

This area is called the concourse. This is where fans can buy a snack or a souvenir. We sell thousands of hot dogs at each game. We also sell lots of hats and T-shirts.

We expect a big crowd for today's game. Our workers have to prepare food, set up souvenir stands, and clean up. We want our building to be ready for the fans.

Large concerts and festivals also take place in stadiums. For these events, the grounds crew rolls a cover onto the grass. The cover protects the playing field from damage.

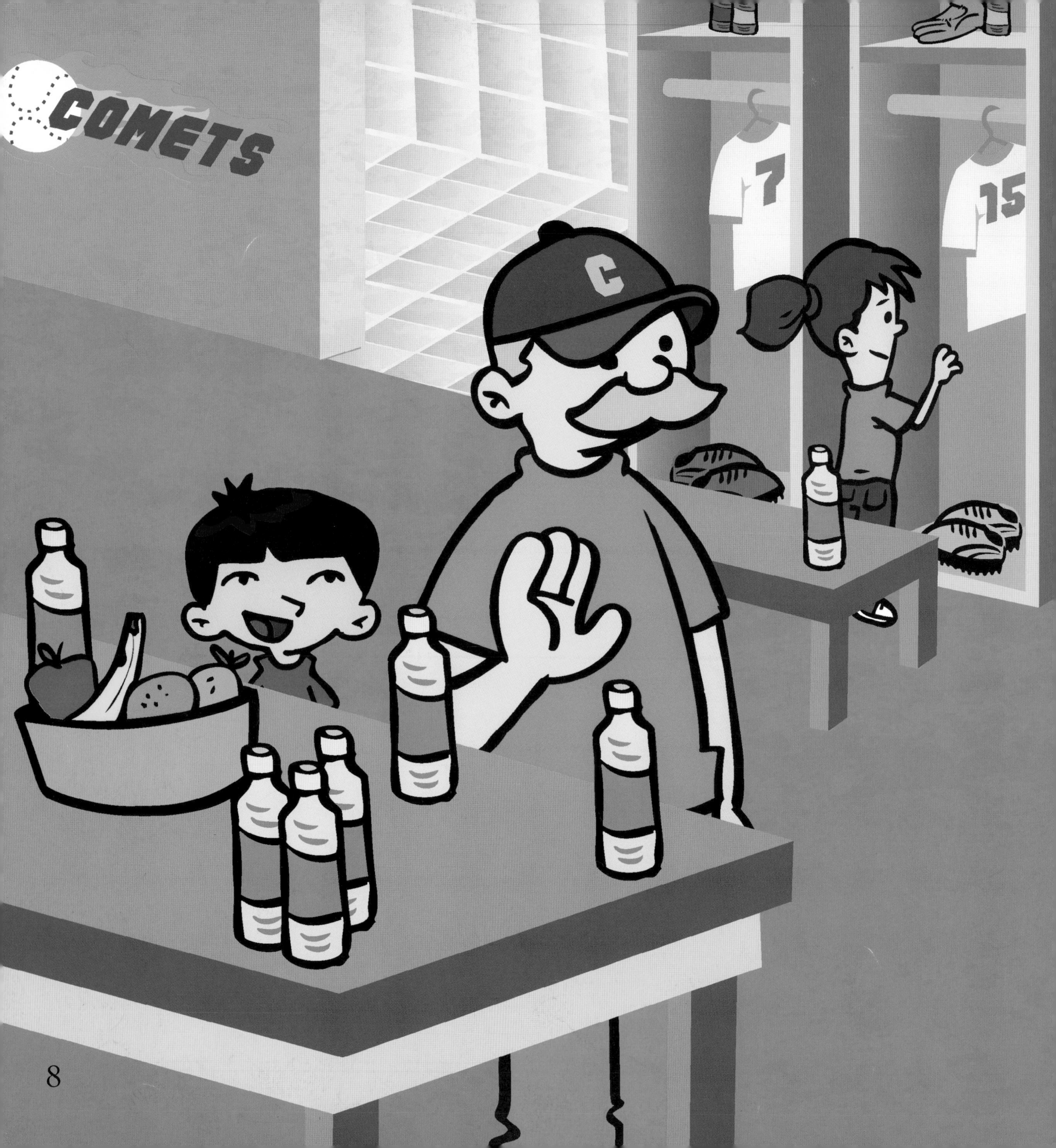
COMETS
C
7
15

This part of the stadium is called the clubhouse. Roy is the clubhouse attendant. Players call him a "clubby." He makes sure uniforms are clean and pressed. He also sets up the pre-game meal, so players have energy to play their best.

Players spend a lot of time in the clubhouse. Before the game, players get into their uniforms here. After the game, they come back to shower and get dressed.

About 50 baseballs are used in every professional baseball game.

9

This is the training room. Julia is the team's trainer. She helps keep the players in good shape. She also helps players get better when they have been injured. Right now, she has to tape up Bobby's sore ankle. Bobby plays centerfield.

10

In the training room, Julia has weights, exercise equipment, and a hot tub that helps players with sore muscles. She also has lots of medical supplies, such as ice packs and bandages.

Baseball managers have private offices. That's where they meet with coaches and choose the lineup. The lineup is the list of which team members will play that day and the order in which they will bat.

This is our dugout. Players sit on the bench here and wait to bat or to take the field. A tunnel under the stands connects the dugout to the clubhouse.

Like a "clubby" in the locker room, bat boys and bat girls prepare the dugout. Batting helmets need to be set out, and bats need to be placed on the rack. Also, water, bubble gum, and sunflower seeds need to be handy for the players.

Lucy and Mitch are our bat girl and bat boy. They stay very busy during the games.

New baseballs can be too shiny and slippery. Umpires, bat boys, and bat girls often rub a little dirt on new baseballs. Adding a little dirt can make them easier to handle.

13

A large grounds crew cares for the field. They keep the grass green and the infield dirt smooth. The grounds crew needs lots of gear, such as rakes, paint, chalk, hoses, and lawn mowers. Some stadiums have artificial turf instead of grass, but even those fields need a lot of care.

Roberto leads our grounds crew. He watered the grass overnight. This morning, his crew mowed the outfield and infield. Now, they are painting the white baselines with a special machine. They make sure the lines are perfectly straight.

The grounds crew uses special lawn mowers to make patterns in the grass. The mowers first cut the grass, then bend it. One pattern the mowers make looks like a checkerboard in the outfield.

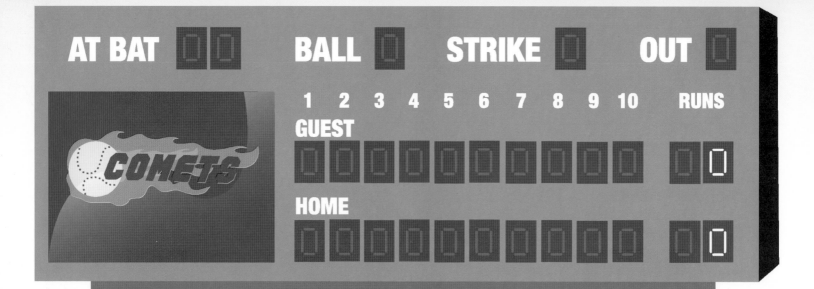

16

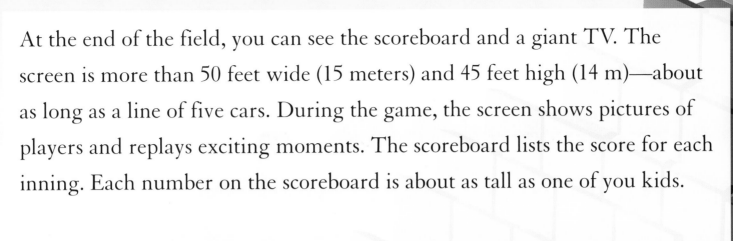

At the end of the field, you can see the scoreboard and a giant TV. The screen is more than 50 feet wide (15 meters) and 45 feet high (14 m)—about as long as a line of five cars. During the game, the screen shows pictures of players and replays exciting moments. The scoreboard lists the score for each inning. Each number on the scoreboard is about as tall as one of you kids.

Now let's head up to the press box. That's a busy place during games.

Thousands of lightbulbs make the scoreboard numbers easy to read, even for fans far across the stadium. Lightbulbs in the scoreboard last a long time. They need changing only about once every two years.

17

This is the press box. Here is the microphone where the radio announcer describes the game and tells people at home what's happening. Over there is one of the cameras used when the game is on TV.

Reporters sit up here and use laptop computers to write their stories about the game. The official scorer sits here, too. It's his or her job to watch and record all of the pitches, runs, hits, and errors.

The press box has a glass window on the front. Reporters and others cans see the whole field while staying warm and dry even on a rainy day.

It is time to find your seats. Your ticket will tell you exactly where to sit. The sections are in alphabetical order around the stadium. The rows and seats are numbered.

I hope you enjoyed your tour of a baseball stadium. The game starts soon. Have fun and cheer hard!

A crowd of 40,000 people can make quite a mess. It can take 50 people about five hours to clean up the stands after a baseball game.

# PLAY BALL

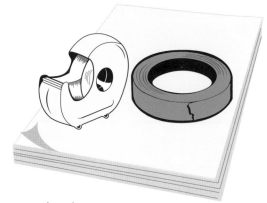

**What you need:**
a large, square piece of paper
a blank piece of white paper
clear tape
colored tape, cut into four 9-inch (23-centimeter) pieces

**What you do:**

1. Fold the blank paper into a triangle, then fold it in half again four more times. You should end up with a small, firm triangle. Tape it closed with clear tape.

2. Place the large piece of paper on a table or flat surface. Create a square with the colored tape, so it looks like a baseball diamond. Start at the bottom of the diamond (home plate). Have Player One place the paper triangle there, on end, and flick it with his or her finger. If the triangle lands outside the tape on the sides, it's considered an out, and Player Two has a turn. If it soars beyond the end of the paper, it's a home run. That player plays again. The first person to hit seven home runs wins.

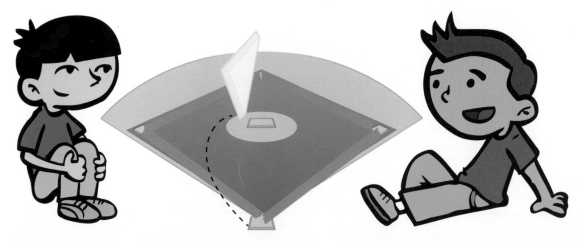

# FUN FACTS

- Chicago's Wrigley Field was the last Major League Baseball stadium to get lights. Until August 8, 1988, no evening games could be played at Wrigley.

- When Raley Field was built in Sacramento, California, it took the work of 1,200 people and nearly a year's time to complete. And that was for a minor-league stadium that seats only 14,000 fans!

- Yankee Stadium in New York is the biggest Major League Baseball stadium, seating 57,545 people. More than 1 million screws were used to build the seats in 1923.

- Fenway Park in Boston is the smallest Major League stadium, with seating for 33,871 people. It is also the oldest ballpark, having opened in 1912.

- A baseball diamond is really a 90-foot (27-meter) square. The bases are exactly 90 feet (27 m) apart.

- There are 30 teams in Major League Baseball and more than 200 in the minor leagues.

# GLOSSARY

clubhouse—the locker room used by a baseball team

concourse—a wide hallway where crowds can gather and move around in a stadium

dugout—a low shelter holding the players' bench; baseball diamonds have one dugout for each team

souvenir—something that is a reminder of a special event

trainer—a person who treats the injuries of a baseball club or another sports team

# TO LEARN MORE

### At the Library

Buckley, James. *Let's Go to the Ballpark*. New York: DK Publishing, 2005.

Hill, Mary. *Let's Go to a Baseball Game*. New York: Children's Press, 2004.

Oxlade, Chris. *Stadiums*. Chicago: Heinemann Library, 2006.

### On the Web

FactHound offers a safe, fun way to find Internet sites related to this book. All of the sites on FactHound have been researched by our staff.

1. Visit *www.facthound.com*
2. Type in this special code for age-appropriate sites: 1404822801
3. Click on the FETCH IT button.

Your trusty FactHound will fetch the best sites for you!

# INDEX

Look for all of the books in the Field Trips series:

*Out and About at ...*

The Apple Orchard 1-4048-0036-0
The Aquarium 1-4048-0298-3
The Bakery 1-4048-0037-9
The Bank 1-4048-1147-8
The Baseball Stadium 1-4048-2280-1
City Hall 1-4048-1146-X
The Dairy Farm 1-4048-0038-7
The Dentist 1-4048-0039-5
The Fire Station 1-4048-2279-8
The Greenhouse 1-4048-2278-X
The Hospital 1-4048-1148-6
The Newspaper 1-4048-1149-4
The Orchestra 1-4048-0040-9
The Planetarium 1-4048-0299-1
The Post Office 1-4048-0294-0
The Public Library 1-4048-1150-8
The Science Center 1-4048-0297-5
The Supermarket 1-4048-0295-9
The Theater 1-4048-2281-X
The United States Mint 1-4048-1151-6
The Vet Clinic 1-4048-0296-7
The Zoo 1-4048-0041-7